Copyright © 2013
ALL RIGHTS RESERV
licensed one copy f
reproduced, redistr.
without prior written permission of the publisher and copyright owner.
Questions regarding permissions or copyrighting may be sent to
support@triviumtestprep.com
Trivium Test Prep is not affiliated with or endorsed by any testing
organization and does not own or claim ownership of any trademarks
of exams or third parties mentioned in this book or title. All test names
(and their acronyms) are trademarks of their respective owners. This
study guide is for general information and does not claim endorsement
by any third party.

Printed in the United States of America.

Congratulations! You are holding in your hands one of the most effective tools for test preparation available. The efficiency of flashcards joined with the convenience and ease of use of a book. We want to offer a quick reminder about how these flashcards are set up and what you can expect. There are three sets of flashcards in this book:

1. Math Flashcards – Starting on page 5, there top (grey) flashcards are mathematics.
2. Verbal Flash Cards – Also starting on page 5, the bottom (white) flash cards are verbal.
3. Science – Starting on page 339, all flash cards from that point forward are Science (both top and bottom).

In either case, the question is on the right page and you simply flip the page to see the answer, just like with a traditional flashcard. We highly suggest working through one set at time, so do all the math or if you want you can start with the bottom set and do all the verbal cards first.

About The Math Flash Cards
These cards will quiz you over different mathematical principles, as well as "mental math" cards. These mental math cards will have simple addition, subtraction, division, etc. The goal is to do them as quickly and accurately as possible. You might wonder why these are included, and the reason is that a majority of points lost on the test are simple mathematical errors, all of which could have been avoided.

Students who rely on their calculator often fail to notice that an input error occurred. By working on these cards, your brain will be primed and ready for the exam. You will answer questions faster and you will make fewer mistakes, both of which equates to a higher score! This seems like "basic" stuff, and it is. The catch is most people fail to work on the basics, and that's why they don't score as high as they would have liked.

About the Verbal Flash Cards
For the verbal cards, you'll have questions testing your knowledge of different components of the English language that you must be familiar with as well as the top "MUST-KNOW" vocabulary words for the test. Remember that with the vocabulary words, the goal is not to memorize the exact definition given here. The point is to know the general meaning of the word. If you find there are words you just can't quite remember when you come back to them, try using them in context. Really! Just use them in a couple sentences and that will help lock them in for future recall.

About the Science Flash Cards
As you noticed, the science flash cards gets its own entire section, both top and bottom. Just like with the math and verbal though, work through only one set at a time, either the top (grey) or the bottom (white). The idea with any flash card is to quickly test your brain to recall knowledge, and get immediate response of whether you were correct or not.

Math Flash Cards

Verbal & Vocabulary Flash Cards

What are the rules for Positive & Negative numbers (adding/subtracting/multiplication/etc)?

What does "denotation" mean?

(+) + (−) = Subtract the two numbers.
  Solution gets the sign of the larger number.
(−) + (−) = Negative number.
(−) * (−) = Positive number.
(−) * (+) = Negative number.
(−) / (−) = Positive number.
(−) / (+) = Negative number.

Denotations mean the literal or primary meaning of a word as found in the dictionary.

What is Greatest Common Factor (GCF)?

What does "connotation" of a word mean?

The greatest factor that divides two numbers.

Example: The GCF of 24 and 18 is 6. 6 is the largest number, or greatest factor, that can divide both 24 and 18.

Connotations are the implied meaning(s) or emotion which the word makes you think.

Example: "Sure," Pam said excitedly, "I'd just love to join your club; it sounds so exciting!"

Now, read this sentence:

"Sure," Pam said sarcastically, "I'd just love to join your club; it sounds so exciting!"

Even though the two sentences only differ by one word, they have completely different meanings. The difference, of course, lies in the words "excitedly" and "sarcastically."

What is the Order of Operations?

What is a Noun?

PEMDAS –
Parentheses/Exponents/Multiply/Divide/Add/Subtract

Perform the operations within parentheses first, and then any exponents. After those steps, perform all multiplication and division. (These are done from left to right, as they appear in the problem) Finally, do all required addition and subtraction, also from left to right as they appear in the problem.

Nouns are people, places, or things. They are typically the subject of a sentence. For example, "The hospital was very clean." The noun is "hospital;" it is the "place."

What are Probabilities?

What are Pronouns?

A probability is found by dividing the number of desired outcomes by the number of possible outcomes. (The piece divided by the whole.)

Example: What is the probability of picking a blue marble if 3 of the 15 marbles are blue?
3/15 = 1/5. The probability is 1 in 5 that a blue marble is picked.

Pronouns essentially "replace" nouns. This allows a sentence to not sound repetitive. Take the sentence: "Sam stayed home from school because Sam was not feeling well." The word "Sam" appears twice in the same sentence. Instead, you can use a pronoun and say, "Sam stayed at home because he did not feel well." Sounds much better, right?

What is the calculation for simple interest?

What are the Most Common Pronouns?

Interest * Principle.

Example: If I deposit $500 into an account with an annual rate of 5%, how much will I have after 2 years?
1st year: 500 + (500*.05) = 525.
2nd year: 525 + (525*.05) = 551.25.

Most Common Pronouns:

- I, me, mine, my
- You, your, yours
- He, him, his
- She, her, hers
- It, its
- We, us, our, ours
- They, them, their, theirs

What is Prime Factorization?

What is a Verb?

Expand to prime number factors.
Example: 104 = 2 * 2 * 2 * 13.

Verbs are the "action" of a sentence; verbs "do" things.

They can, however, be quite tricky. Depending on the subject of a sentence, the tense of the word (past, present, future, etc.), and whether or not they are regular or irregular, verbs have many variations.

Example: "He runs to second base." The verb is "runs." This is a "regular verb."

Example: "I am 7 years old." The verb in this case is "am." This is an "irregular verb."

What is Absolute Value?

What are Adjectives?

The absolute value of a number is its distance from zero, not its value.

So in $|x| = a$, "x" will equal "-a" as well as "a." Likewise, $|3| = 3$, and $|-3| = 3$.

Equations with absolute values will have two answers. Solve each absolute value possibility separately. All solutions must be checked into the original equation.

Adjectives are words that describe a noun and give more information. Take the sentence: "The boy hit the ball." If you want to know more about the noun "boy," then you could use an adjective to describe it. "The little boy hit the ball." An adjective simply provides more information about a noun or subject in a sentence.

Describe Mean, Median, and Mode?

What is an Adverb?

Mean is a math term for "average." Total all terms and divide by the number of terms.

Median is the middle number of a given set, found after the numbers have all been put in numerical order. In the case of a set of even numbers, the middle two numbers are averaged.

Mode is the number which occurs most frequently within a given set.

Adverbs are similar to adjectives in that they provide more information; however, they describe verbs, adjectives, and even other adverbs. They do not describe nouns – that's an adjective's job.

Take the sentence: "The doctor said she hired a new employee."

It would give more information to say: "The doctor said she recently hired a new employee." Now we know more about how the action was executed. Adverbs typically describe when or how something has happened, how it looks, how it feels, etc.

What is an Arithmetic Sequence?

What is a Root?

Each term is equal to the previous term plus x.

Example: 2, 5, 8, 11.
 2 + 3 = 5; 5 + 3 = 8 ... etc.
 x = 3.

Roots are the building blocks of all words. Every word is either a root itself or has a root. Just as a plant cannot grow without roots, neither can vocabulary, because a word must have a root to give it meaning.

Example: The test instructions were *unclear*.

The root is what is left when you strip away all the prefixes and suffixes from a word. In this case, take away the prefix "un-," and you have the root clear.

What is a Geometric Sequence?

What are Prefixes?

Each term is equal to the previous term multiplied by x.

Example: 2, 4, 8, 16.
    x = 2.

Prefixes are syllables added to the beginning of a word and suffixes are syllables added to the end of the word. Both carry assigned meanings. The common name for prefixes and suffixes is affixes.

Let's use the word *prefix* itself as an example:

Fix means to place something securely.
Pre means before.
Prefix means to place something before or in front.

What is the formula for Percent? Part? Whole?

What are Suffixes?

Part = Percent * Whole.
Percent = Part / Whole.
Whole = Part / Percent.

Example: Jim spent 30% of his paycheck at the fair. He spent $15 for a hat, $30 for a shirt, and $20 playing games. How much was his check? (Round to nearest dollar.)

Whole = 65 / .30 = $217.00.

Suffixes come after the root of a word.

>   Example: Feminism

>   Femin is a root. It means female, woman.

>   -ism means act, practice or process.

>   Feminism is the defining and establishing of equal political, economic, and social rights for women.

What are the formulas for Percent Change, Increase, and Decrease?

"The medication must be properly administered to the patient."

Which of the words in the above sentence is an adverb?
        a. Medication.
        b. Properly.
        c. Administered.
        d. Patient.

Percent Change = Amount of Change / Original Amount * 100.

Percent Increase = (New Amount − Original Amount) / Original Amount * 100.

Percent Decrease = (Original Amount − New Amount) / Original Amount * 100.

Amount Increase (or Decrease) = Original Price * Percent Markup (or Markdown).

Original Price = New Price / (Whole - Percent Markdown [or Markup]).

Answer: b)

"Properly" is the adverb which describes the verb "administered."

What are the formulas for Repeated Percent Change?

"The old man had trouble walking if he did not have his walker and had a long way to go."

What is the subject of the sentence?
        a. Walker.
        b. His.
        c. Trouble.
        d. Man.

Increase: Final amount = Original Amount * (1 + rate) # of changes.

Decrease: Final Amount = Original Amount * (1 – rate) # of changes.

Example: The weight of a tube of toothpaste decreases by 3% each time it is used. If it weighed 76.5 grams when new, what is its weight in grams after 15 uses?

Final amount = 76.5 * (1 - .3)15.
76.5 * (.97)15 = 48.44 grams.

Answer: d)
Although there are other nouns in the sentence, the "man" is the subject.

What is Combined Average?

"The boy decided ___ would ride his bike now that the sun was shining."

Which of the following pronouns completes the sentence?
        a. His.
        b. Him.
        c. He.
        d. They.

Weigh each average individual average before determining the sum.

Example: If Cory averaged 3 hits per game during the summer and 2 hits per game during the fall and played 7 games in the summer and 8 games in the fall, what was his hit average overall?

>Summer: 3 * 7 = 21.
>Fall: 2 * 8 = 16.
>Sum: 21 + 16 = 37.
>
>Total number of games: 7 + 8 = 15.
>Calculate average: 37/15 = ~ 2.47 hits/game.

Answer: c)
"He" is the correct answer; the other pronouns are possessive or otherwise in the wrong tense.

How do you solve Ratios?

"The impatient student hurried through the test and failed as a result."

Which word is an adjective?
        a. Hurried.
        b. Result.
        c. Impatient.
        d. Student.

To solve a ratio, simply find the equivalent fraction. To distribute a whole across a ratio:

Total all parts.
Divide the whole by the total number of parts.
Multiply quotient by corresponding part of ratio.

Example: There are 90 voters in a room, and they are either Democrat or Republican. The ratio of Democrats to Republicans is 5:4. How many Republicans are there?

$$5 + 4 = 9.$$
$$90 / 9 = 10.$$
$$10 * 4 = 40 \text{ Republicans}.$$

Answer: c)
"Impatient" describes the noun "student."

What are Direct Proportions?

Correct the verb: "The nurse decided it were a good time to follow up with a patient about their medication."
    a. Was.
    b. Is.
    c. Has.
    d. No error.

Corresponding ratio parts change in the same direction (increase/decrease).

Answer: a)
"Was" is the correct answer; the other choices are in the wrong tense.

What are Indirect Proportions?

To take precaution is to:
    a. Prepare before doing something.
    b. Remember something that happened earlier.
    c. Become aware of something for the first time.
    d. Try to do something again.

Corresponding ratio parts change in opposite directions (as one part increases the other decreases).

Example: A train traveling 120 miles takes 3 hours to get to its destination. How long will it take if the train travels 180 miles?

120 mph: 180 mph is to x hours: 3 hours. (Write as fraction and cross multiply.)
    120/3 = 180/x.
    540 = 120x.
    x = 4.5 hours.

Answer: a) Prepare before doing something.
Pre- means before; to take caution is to be careful or take heed.

What is the formula for the Root of a Product?

To reorder a list is to:
    a. Use the same order again.
    b. Put the list in a new order.
    c. Get rid of the list.
    d. Find the list.

$$\sqrt[n]{a \cdot b} = \sqrt[n]{a} \cdot \sqrt[n]{b}.$$

Answer: b) Put the list in a new order.
Re- means again. In this case, order means organize. Reorder then means to organize the list again or to put the list into a different order.

What is the formula for the Root of a Quotient?

An antidote to a disease is:
   a. Something that is part of the disease.
   b. Something that works against the disease.
   c. Something that makes the disease worse.
   d. Something that has nothing to do with the disease.

$$\sqrt[n]{\frac{a}{b}} = \frac{\sqrt[n]{a}}{\sqrt[n]{b}}.$$

Answer: b) Something that works against the disease.
The prefix anti- means against. An antidote is something that works against a disease or a poison.

What is the formula for Fractional Exponents?

Someone who is multiethnic:
    a. Likes only certain kinds of people.
    b. Lives in the land of his or her birth.
    c. Is from a different country.
    d. Has many different ethnicities.

$$\sqrt[n]{a^m} = a^{m/n}$$

Answer: d) Has many different ethnicities.

The prefix multi- means many. Someone who is multiethnic has relatives from many different ethnic groups.

What is formula for the Fundamental Counting Principle?

Someone who is misinformed has been:
  a. Taught something new.
  b. Told the truth.
  c. Forgotten.
  d. Given incorrect information.

(The number of possibilities of an event happening) * (the number of possibilities of another event happening) = the total number of possibilities.

Example: If you take a multiple choice test with 5 questions, with 4 answer choices for each question, how many test result possibilities are there?

Solution: Question 1 has 4 choices; question 2 has 4 choices; etc.
4 *4 * 4 * 4 * 4 (one for each question) = 1024 possible test results.

Answer: d) Given incorrect information.

Mis- means opposite, and to be informed is to have the correct information.

What are Literal Equations?

Define abate:

Equations with more than one variable. Solve in terms of one variable first.

Example: Solve for y: $4x + 3y = 3x + 2y$.

Combine like terms: $3y - 2y = 4x - 2x$.

Solve for y: $y = 2x$.

become less in amount or intensity

What are Linear Systems?

Define abdicate:

A linear system requires the solving of two literal equations simultaneously. There are two different methods (Substitution and Addition) that can be used to solve linear systems.

to give up or leave

What are Linear Equations?

Define aberration:

An equation for a straight line. The variable CANNOT have an exponent, square roots, cube roots, etc.

Example: $y = 2x + 1$ is a straight line, with "1" being the y-intercept, and "2" being the positive slope.

a state or condition very different from the norm

What are Inequalities? How are they solved?

Define abbreviate:

Inequalities are solved like linear and algebraic equations, except the sign must be reversed when dividing by a negative number.

Example: $-7x + 2 < 6 - 5x$.

Step 1 – Combine like terms: $-2x < 4$.
Step 2 – Solve for x. (Reverse the sign): $x > -2$.

to shorten or abridge

What are the rules for exponents?

Define abstain:

Rule	Example
$x^0 = 1$	$5^0 = 1$
$x^1 = x$	$5^1 = 5$
$x^a \cdot x^b = x^{a+b}$	$5^2 * 5^3 = 5^5$
$(xy)^a = x^a y^a$	$(5*6)^2 = 5^2 * 6^2 = 25 * 36$
$(x^a)^b = x^{ab}$	$(5^2)^3 = 5^6$
$(x/y)^a = x^a/y^a$	$(10/5)^2 = 10^2/5^2 = 100/25$
$x^a/y^b = x^{a-b}$	$5^4/5^3 = 5^1 = 5$ (remember $x \neq 0$)
$x^{1/a} = \sqrt[a]{x}$	$25^{1/2} = \sqrt[2]{25} = 5$
$x^{-a} = \frac{1}{x^a}$	$5^{-2} = \frac{1}{5^2} = \frac{1}{25}$ (remember $x \neq 0$)

choose to avoid or not participate

What are Permutations?

Define adversity:

The number of ways a set number of items can be arranged. Recognized by the use of a factorial (n!), with n being the number of items.

If n = 3, then 3! = 3 * 2 * 1 = 6. If you need to arrange n number of things but x number are alike, then n! is divided by x!

Example: How many different ways can the letters in the word balance be arranged?

Solution: There are 7 letters, so n! = 7! But 2 letters are the same, so x! = 2! Set up the equation:
(7* 6* 5* 4* 3* 2* 1)/(2* 1) = 2540 ways.

a state of burden or hardship

How do you calculate the number of possible combinations?

Define adulation:

To calculate total number of possible combinations, use the formula: $n!/r!(n-r)!$
Where n = # of objects; and r = # of objects selected at a time.

Example: If seven people are selected in groups of three, how many different combinations are possible?

Solution:
$(7* 6* 5* 4* 3* 2* 1)/((3*2* 1)(7-3)) = 210$ possible combinations.

Excessive praise and flattery

How do you factor Quadratics?

Define aesthetic:

Factoring: converting $ax^2 + bx + c$ to factored form.
Find two numbers that are factors of c and whose sum is b.
Example: Factor $2x^2 + 12x + 18 = 0$.

Factor out a common monomial: $2(x^2 - 6x + 9)$.
Find two factors of 9 and sum to -6: $2(x -)(x -\_)$.
Fill in the binomials: $2(x - 3)(x - 3)$.

To solve, set each to = 0: $x - 3 = 0; x = 3$.

If the equation cannot be factored (there are no two factors of c that sum to = b), the quadratic formula is used. $x = (-b \pm \sqrt{b^2 - 4ac})/2a$

concerning or an appreciation of beauty, art, or design

What is an Acute Angle?

Define amicable:

Angle that measures less than 90°.

characterized by friendship and good will

What is an Acute Triangle?

Define amenable:

Each angle measures less than 90 °.

open to suggestion and willing to follow advice

What is an Obtuse Angle?

Define antiquated:

Measures greater than 90°.

obsolete, old, out of fashion

What is an Obtuse Triangle?

Define anachronistic:

One angle measures greater than 90°.

out of date or belonging to another time

What are Adjacent Angles?

Define anecdote:

Angles sharing a side and a vertex.

a short story or account of an event

What are Complementary Angles?

Define antagonist:

Adjacent angles that sum to 90°.

An opponent; someone in conflict with the hero of a story

What are Supplementary Angles?

Define arid:

Adjacent angles that sum to 180°.

lacking water or rainfall

What are Vertical Angles?

Define asylum:

Angles that are opposite of each other. They are always congruent (equal in measure).

shelter from danger or hardship

What is an Equilateral Triangle?

Define assiduous:

All angles of the triangle are equal.

Very careful and hardworking

What is an Isosceles Triangle?

Define benevolent:

Two sides and two angles are equal.

showing sympathy, understanding, and generosity

What does Scalene mean?

Define bias:

No equal angles.

an unfair preference of dislike of something

What are Parallel Lines?

Define boisterous:

Lines that will never intersect. Y ∥ X means line Y is parallel to line X.

Rough, rowdy, and unruly

Describe Perpendicular lines?

Define brazen:

Lines that intersect or cross to form 90° angles.

Bold or unrestrained by normal standards

What is a Transversal Line?

Define brusque:

A line that crosses parallel lines.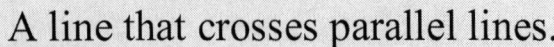

attitude of shortness, rudeness; gruff

What is a Bisector?

Define camaraderie:

Any line that cuts a line segment, angle, or polygon exactly in half.

the quality of familiarity or friendship

What is a Polygon?

Define capacious:

Any enclosed plane shape with three or more connecting sides (ex. a triangle).

large in size or capacity

What is a Regular Polygon?

Define censure:

Has all equal sides and equal angles (ex. square).

Disapproval or several criticize

What is an Arc?

Define circuitous:

A portion of a circle's edge.

lengthy due to being indirect or roundabout

What is a Chord?

Define clairvoyant:

A line segment that connects two different points on a circle.

a person with the ability to read minds or see the future

What is a Tangent?

Define clandestine:

Something that touches a circle at only one point without crossing through it.

secret and concealed

What is the formula for the Sum of Angles?

Define collaborate:

The sum of angles of a polygon can be calculated using: $(n-1)180°$
when n = the number of sides.

work together on a common project

What are Trapezoids?

Define collateral:

Four-sided polygon, in which the bases (and only the bases) are parallel.

adjoining or accompanying

What is an Isosceles Trapezoid?

Define compassion:

Base angles are congruent.

awareness and sympathy for the suffering of others

What is a Rhombus?

Define compromise:

Four-sided polygon, in which all four sides are congruent and opposite sides are parallel.

an accommodation in which both sides make concessions

What are the formulas for the Area and Perimeter of a Rhombus?

Define condescending:

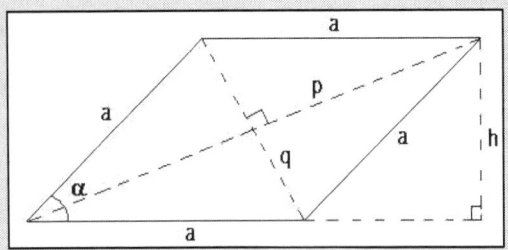

$Perimeter = 4a$

$Area = a^2 \sin \alpha = a * h = \dfrac{1}{2} pq$

$4a^2 = p^2 + q^2$

an attitude of superiority or being snobby towards others

What are the formulas for the Area and Perimeter of a Rectangle?

Define conditional:

$d = \sqrt{a^2 + h^2}$

$a = \sqrt{d^2 - h^2}$

$h = \sqrt{d^2 - a^2}$

$Perimeter = 2a + 2h$

$Area = a \cdot h$

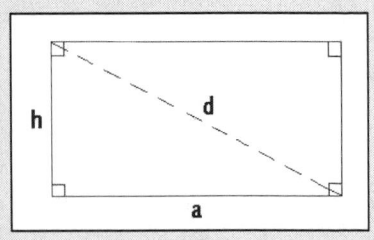

dependent on something else being done

What are the formulas for the Area and Perimeter of a Square?

Define conformist:

$d = a\sqrt{2}$

$Perimeter = 4a = 2d\sqrt{2}$

$Area = a^2 = \dfrac{1}{2}d^2$

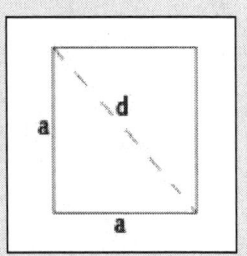

someone who follows standards or rules of conduct

What are the formulas for the Area of a Circle?

Define congregation:

$d = 2r$

$Perimeter = 2\pi r = \pi d$

$Area = \pi r^2$

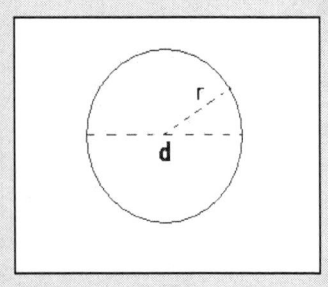

a gathering or crowd of people

What are the formulas for the Area and Volume of a Cube?

Define convergence:

$r = a\sqrt{2}$

$d = a\sqrt{3}$

$Area = 6a^2$

$Volume = a^3$

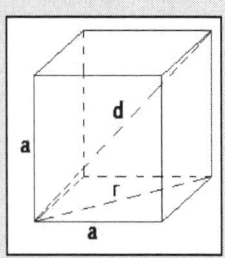

the act of coming together; joining of parts

What are the formulas for the Area and Volume of a Cuboid?

Define cursory:

$$d = \sqrt{a^2 + b^2 + c^2}$$
$$A = 2(ab + ac + bc)$$
$$V = abc$$

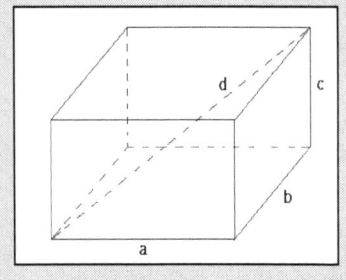

quickly and superficially done

What are the formulas for the Area and Volume of a Pyramid?

Define copious:

$$A_{lateral} = a\sqrt{h^2 + \left(\frac{b}{2}\right)^2} + b\sqrt{h^2 + \left(\frac{a}{2}\right)^2}$$

$$d = \sqrt{a^2 + b^2}$$

$$A_{base} = ab$$

$$A_{total} = A_{lateral} + A_{base}$$

$$V = \frac{1}{3}abh$$

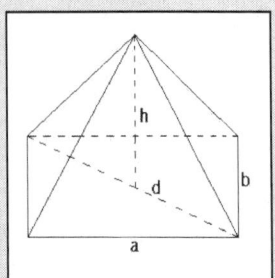

abundant and plentiful

What are the formulas for the Area and Volume of a Cylinder?

Define concise:

$d = 2r$

$A_{surface} = 2\pi r h$

$A_{base} = 2\pi r^2$

$Area = A_{surface} + A_{base}$

$\qquad = 2\pi r (h + r)$

$Volume = \pi r^2 h$

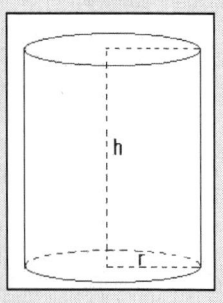

brief, condensed

What are the formulas for the Areas and Volume of a Cone?

Define deleterious:

$d = 2r$

$A_{surface} = \pi r s$

$A_{base} = \pi r^2$

$Area = A_{surface} + A_{base}$

$\qquad = 2\pi r (h + r)$

$Volume = \dfrac{1}{3} \pi r^2 h$

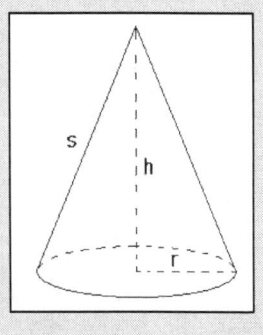

harmful or deadly to living things

$9^2 = ?$

Define demagogue:

81

a leader who gains power by appealing to emotions and prejudices

$10^2 = ?$

Define deride:

100

mock, ridicule, laugh at

$11^2 = ?$

Define despot:

121

to rule with oppression and tyranny

$12^2 = ?$

Define deter:

144

to prevent or discourage

$1! = ?$

Define digression:

1

a deviation or detour from the central topic or focus

$2! = ?$

Define diligent:

2

persistent and hardworking

$3! = ?$

Define discredit:

6

to cause doubt or to harm the reputation of someone

$$4! = ?$$

Define disdain:

24

lack of respect or intense dislike

$5! = ?$

Define divergent:

120

to move apart in different directions

decimal of 1/8 = ?

Define elusive:

0.125

hard to find or catch

decimal of 3/8 = ?

Define empathy:

0.375

understanding of another's feelings

decimal of 5/8 = ?

Define emulate:

0.625

try to equal someone or something,
such as by imitating

decimal of 7/8 = ?

Define enhance:

0.875

to improve; increase clarity

$5*12 = ?$

Define enervating:

60

causing debilitation or weakness

$6*12 = ?$

Define ephemeral:

72

lasting only for a short period of time

$7*12 = ?$

Define evanescent:

84

disappearing after a short time and quickly forgotten

$7*9 = ?$

Define exasperate:

63

worsen, make angry or frustrate

8*9 = ?

Define exemplary:

72

worthy of imitation, setting the example

14*5 = ?

Define extenuating:

70

diminish the seriousness of something

14*6 = ?

Define florid:

84

ornate in wording or style

$7 * 14 = ?$

Define forbearance:

98

a delay in enforcing legal right;
refraining from acting

$8*14 = ?$

Define fortitude:

112

strength and endurance during a difficult situation

9*14 = ?

Define fortuitous:

126

occurring by happy chance

$7*6 = ?$

Define foster:

42

providing parental care or to develop something

7*7 = ?

Define fraught:

49

filled with or accompanied by
problems or difficulties

$7*8 = ?$

Define frugal:

56

avoiding waste, thrifty

4*8 = ?

Define gullible:

32

easily deceived or tricked

33*4 = ?

Define garble:

132

confuse, not understandable

33*5 = ?

Define hackneyed:

ordinary because of overuse

30*4 = ?

Define haughty:

120

acting arrogant or superior to others

24*6 = ?

Define hedonism:

144

seeking of selfish and sensual pleasures

$18*3 = ?$

Define hiatus:

54

a break, vacation from, or pause

19*3 = ?

Define hypothesis:

57

a theory that has not yet been tested or investigated

$17*3 = ?$

Define hyperbole:

51

exaggerating, making something more than it is

16*3 = ?

Define heresy:

48

against orthodox opinion or belief

$21*3 = ?$

Define impair:

63

to weaken or harm

$22*4 = ?$

Define impetuous:

88

undue haste without thought of consequences

$72/8 = ?$

Define impute:

9

to give credit of a usually undesirable action

$72/9 = ?$

Define imminent:

8

very likely going to happen

72/2 = ?

Define incompatible:

36

unable to be or work together

68/4 = ?

Define inconsequential:

17

something without importance or significance

68/2 = ?

Define inevitable:

34

impossible to avoid or prevent from happening

$64/4 = ?$

Define intrepid:

16

courageous and bold, without fear

$64/8 = ?$

Define integrity:

8

doing what is right, honest, or decent

58/2 = ?

Define intuitive:

29

to know by instinct alone

$54/3 = ?$

Define innocuous:

18

harmless

48/4 = ?

Define jubilation:

12

a feeling of extreme rejoicing and celebration

48/8 = ?

Define lobbyist:

6

someone who is paid to lobby, or persuade, political representatives, usually of a single particular issue.

$42/2 = ?$

Define longevity:

21

the property of having a long life

$36/12 = ?$

Define larceny:

3

theft, stealing

$120/4 = ?$

Define languid:

30

tired and slow

165/33 = ?

Define mundane:

5

common place, ordinary, or boring

104/13 = ?

Define nonchalant:

8

calm and unconcerned

96/12 = ?

Define novice:

8

a beginner, inexperienced

108/9 = ?

Define opulent:

12

rich and superior in quality

132/12 = ?

Define orator:

11

someone who delivers a speech or oration

144/12 = ?

Define ostentatious:

12

an intended and purposeful show of wealth intended to impress others

65/5 = ?

Define obsess:

13

always thinking about something constantly

$$78/6 = ?$$

Define paradox:

13

appearing conflicting or contradictory

$72/8 = ?$

Define parched:

9

lack of moisture and dried out by heat or sun

$70/5 = ?$

Define pragmatic:

14

concerned with practical matters and results

84/14 = ?

Define perfidious:

6

disloyal, not able to be trusted

$98/14 = ?$

Define precocious:

7

showing advanced development or maturity at an early age

$112/8 = ?$

Define ponder:

14

think over, consider

42/7 = ?

Define pretentious:

6

acting more important or special than what is deserved

$49/7 = ?$

Define procrastinate:

7

to postpone doing something that needs to be done

$56/7 = ?$

Define prosaic:

8

lacking wit or imagination

32/8 = ?

Define prosperity:

4

the condition of being wealthy or successful

18+29 = ?

Define provocative:

47

purposefully exciting, arousing, or annoying someone

17+27 = ?

Define prudent:

44

careful and sensible; using good judgment

$19+56=?$

Define querulous:

75

always complaining or whining

25+42 = ?

Define rancorous:

67

having deeply held and long lasting resentment

$22+35 = ?$

Define reclusive:

57

withdrawn and alone from the world

37+28 = ?

Define reconciliation:

65

the end of conflict and reestablishing relationships or friendship

34+52 = ?

Define renovation:

86

repairing and restoring back to original or better state

35+17 = ?

Define restrained:

52

showing control and not giving into emotion or anger

18-56 = ?

Define respite:

-38

a break or intermission

25-42 = ?

Define resilient:

-17

quick to recover

22-45 = ?

Define reverence:

-23

a feeling of deep respect for someone or something

36-28 = ?

Define sagacity:

8

sound knowledge, judgment, and foresight

35-52 = ?

Define scrutinize:

-17

examine closely and carefully

35-17 = ?

Define spontaneous:

18

done with impulse and not as a result
of planning

78-13 = ?

Define spurious:

65

something not genuine or authentic, as it might be claimed to be

67-25 = ?

Define submissive:

42

giving in to or following the authority
and demands of others

67-19 = ?

Define substantiate:

48

to confirm or prove something is true and valid

62-14 = ?

Define subtle:

48

understated and not obvious

63-19 = ?

Define superficial:

44

shallow in character and attitude, only concerned with things on the surface

57-19 = ?

Define superfluous:

38

more than is needed, desired, or necessary

In a class of 42 students, 18 are boys. Two girls get transferred to another school. What percent of students remaining are girls?
a) 14%.
b) 16%.
c) 52.4%.
d) 60%.
e) None of the above.

Define terse:

Answer: e)
The entire class has 42 students, 18 of which are boys, meaning 42 - 18 = 24 is the number of girls. Out of these 24 girls, 2 leave; so 22 girls are left. The total number of students is now 42 - 2 = 40.
22/40 * 100 = 55%.

Reminder: If you forget to subtract 2 from the total number of students, you will end up with 60% as the answer. Sometimes you may calculate an answer that has been given as a choice; it can still be incorrect. Always check your answer.

to the point, concise

A sweater goes on sale for 30% off. If the original price was $70, what is the discounted price?
 a) $48.
 b) $49.
 c) $51.
 d) $65.
 e) $52.

Define transient:

Answer: b)
New price = original price * (1 − discount) →
new price = 70(1-.3) = 49.

lasting for only a short time or duration

If test A is taken 5 times with an average result of 21, and test B is taken 13 times with an average result of 23, what is the combined average?
 a) 22.24.
 b) 22.22.
 c) 22.00.
 d) 22.44.
 e) 24.22.

Define trite:

Answer : d)

If test A avg = 21 for 5 tests, then sum of test A results = 21 * 5 = 105.
If test B avg = 23 for 13 tests, then sum of test B results = 23 * 13 = 299.
So total result = 299 + 105 = 404.
Average of all tests = 404/(5 + 13) = 404/18 = 22.44.

dull, common

A set of data has 12 entries. The average of the first 6 entries is 12, the average of the next two entries is 20, and the average of the remaining entries is 4. What is the average of the entire data set?
   a) 10.
   b) 10.67.
   c) 11.
   d) 12.67.
   e) 10.5.

Define timorous:

Answer: b)
- The average of the first 6 points is 12 → $s_1/6 = 12$ → $s_1 = 72$; s_1 is the sum of the first 6 points.
- The average of the next 2 points is 20 → $s_2/2 = 20$ → $s_2 = 40$; s_2 is the sum of the next 2 points.
- The average of the remaining 4 points is 4 → $s_3/4 = 4$ → $s_3 = 16$; s_3 is the sum of the last 4 points.
- The sum of all the data points = 72 + 40 + 16 = 128. The average = 128/12 = 10.67.

cowardly, fearful

The number 568cd should be divisible by 2, 5, and 7. What are the values of the digits c and d?
   a) 56835.
   b) 56830.
   c) 56860.
   d) 56840.
   e) 56800.

Define vindicate:

Answer: d)

If the number is divisible by 2, *d* should be even. If the number is divisible by 5, then *b* has to equal 0.

Start by making both variables 0 and dividing by the largest factor, 7. 56800/7 = 8114.

2 from 56800 is 56798, a number divisible by 2 and 7.

Next add a multiple of 7 that turns the last number to a 0. 6 * 7 = 42. 56798 + 42 = 56840, which is divisible by 2, 5, and 7.

proving someone or something
innocent and free of blame or guilt

Carla is 3 times older than her sister Megan. Eight years ago, Carla was 18 years older than her sister. What is Megan's age?
    a) 10.
    b) 8.
    c) 9.
    d) 6.
    e) 5.

Define venerate:

Answer: c)
Carla's age is c; Megan's age is m. $c = 3m$; $c - 8 = m - 8 + 18$.

Substitute $3m$ for c in equation 2 → $3m - 8 = m + 10$ → $m = 9$.

to regard with much respect

If $x < 5$ and $y < 6$, then $x + y$ __?__ 11.
   a) <
   b) >
   c) ≤
   d) ≥
   e) =

Define wary:

Answer: a)
Choice **a)** will always be true, while the other choices can never be true.

Answer: b)
$25x^2 - 40x + 32 < 22$ → $25x^2 - 40x + 16 < 6$ → $(5x - 4)^2 < 6$ → $5x - 4 < 6$.

$x = 2$, so x has to be all numbers less than 2 for this inequality to work.

to be cautious or suspicious

Which of the following is true about the inequality $25x^2 - 40x - 32 < 22$?
   a) There are no solutions.
   b) There is a set of solutions.
   c) There is 1 solution only.
   d) There are 2 solutions.
   e) There are 3 solutions.

Define abut:

Answer: b)
$25x^2 - 40x + 32 < 22$ → $25x^2 - 40x + 16 < 6$ → $(5x - 4)^2 < 6$ → $5x - 4 < 6$.

$x = 2$, so x has to be all numbers less than 2 for this inequality to work.

To touch at the end or boundaries

Car A starts at 3:15 PM and travels straight to its destination at a constant speed of 50 mph. If it arrives at 4:45 PM, how far did it travel?
 a) 70 miles.
 b) 75 miles.
 c) 65 miles.
 d) 40 miles.
 e) 105 miles.

Define baffle:

Answer: b)
The time between 3:15 PM and 4:45 PM = 1.5 hours. 1.5 * 50 = 75.

Reminder: half an hour is written as .5 of an hour, not .3 of an hour, even though on a clock a half hour is 30 minutes.

To foil or frustrate.

What is the area, in square feet, of the triangle whose sides have lengths equal to 3, 4, and 5 feet?

a) 6 square feet.
b) 7 square feet.
c) 4 square feet.
d) 5 square feet.
e) 8 square feet.

Define benevolence:

Answer: a)
The Pythagorean triple (special right triangle property) means the two shorter sides form a right triangle.

$1/2 bh = A$. So, $(1/2)(3)(4) = 6$.

Any act of kindness or well-doing

In the following figure, where AE bisects line BC, and angles AEC and AEB are both right angles, what is the length of AB?

a) 1 cm.
b) 2 cm.
c) 3 cm.
d) 4 cm.
e) 5 cm.

BC = 6 cm
AD = 3 cm
CD = 4 cm

Define blemish:

Answer: e)
$AB^2 = AC^2 = AD2 + CD^2 \rightarrow AB^2 = 3^2 + 4^2 \rightarrow AB = 5$.

A mark that mars beauty.

The wardrobe of a studio contains 4 hats, 3 suits, 5 shirts, 2 pants, and 3 pairs of shoes. How many different ways can these items be put together?
   a) 60.
   b) 300.
   c) 360.
   d) 420.
   e) 500.

Define botany:

Answer: c)
The number of ways = 4 * 3 * 5 * 2 * 3 = 360.

The science that treats of plants.

For lunch, you have a choice between chicken fingers or cheese sticks for an appetizer; turkey, chicken, or veal for the main course; cake or pudding for dessert; and either Coke or Pepsi for a beverage. How many choices of possible meals do you have?
    a) 16.
    b) 24.
    c) 34.
    d) 36.
    e) 8.

Define Braggart:

Answer: b)
Multiply the possible number of choices for each item from which you can choose.

2 * 3 * 2 * 2 = 24.

A vain boaster.

A class has 50% more boys than girls. What is the ratio of boys to girls?
   a) 4:3.
   b) 3:2.
   c) 5:4.
   d) 10:7.
   e) 7:5.

Define Cajole:

Answer: b)
The ratio of boys to girls is 150:100, or 3:2.

To impose on or dupe by flattering speech.

A car can travel 30 miles on 4 gallons of gas. If the gas tank has a capacity of 16 gallons, how far can it travel if the tank is ¾ full?
   a) 120 miles.
   b) 90 miles.
   c) 60 miles.
   d) 55 miles.
   e) 65 miles.

Define Candor:

Answer: b)
A full tank has 16 gallons → 3/4 of the tank = 12 gallons. The car can travel 30 miles on 4 gallons, so 12 gallons would take the car 12 * 30/4 = 90 miles.

The quality of frankness or outspokenness.

What is the value of $f(x) = (x^2 - 25)/(x + 5)$ when $x = 0$?

    a) -1.
    b) -2.
    c) -3.
    d) -4.
    e) -5.

Define Capitulate:

Answer: e)
We know $(x^2 - 25) = (x + 5)(x - 5)$.

So $(x^2 - 25)/(x + 5) = x - 5$. At $x = 0, f(0) = -5$.

To surrender or stipulate terms.

Four years from now, John will be twice as old as Sally will be. If Sally was 10 eight years ago, how old is John?
- a) 35.
- b) 40.
- c) 45.
- d) 50.
- e) 55.

Define Castigate:

Answer: b)
Let j be John's age and s be Sally's age.

$j + 4 = 2(s + 4)$.

$s - 8 = 10 \rightarrow s = 18$.

So $j + 4 = 2(18 + 4) \rightarrow j = 40$.

To punish

Science Section Flash Cards start on the next page!

From this point forward, both top and bottom sets are only Science.

Science Flash Card Set #1

Science Flash Card Set #2

What are Organic molecules?

What are Inorganic molecules?

Organic molecules are from living organisms. Organic molecules contain **carbon-hydrogen bonds**.

Inorganic molecules come from non-living resources. They do not contain carbon-hydrogen bonds.

What are Carbohydrates?

What are Lipids?

Carbohydrates consist of only hydrogen, oxygen, and carbon atoms. They are the most abundant single class of organic substances found in nature. Carbohydrate molecules provide many basic necessities such as: fiber, vitamins, and minerals; structural components for organisms, especially plants; and, perhaps most importantly, energy. Our bodies break down carbohydrates to make **glucose**: a sugar used to produce that energy which our bodies need in order to operate. Brain cells are exclusively dependent upon a constant source of glucose molecules.

Lipids, commonly known as fats, are molecules with two functions:

1. They are stored as an energy reserve.

2. They provide a protective cushion for vital organs.

In addition to those two functions, lipids also combine with other molecules to form essential compounds, such as **phospholipids,** which form the membranes around cells. Lipids also combine with other molecules to create naturally-occurring **steroid** hormones, like the hormones estrogen and testosterone.

What are Proteins?

What is Nucleic Acid?

Proteins are large molecules which our bodies' cells need in order to function properly. Consisting of **amino acids,** proteins aid in maintaining and creating many aspects of our cells: cellular structure, function, and regulation, to name a few. Proteins also work as neurotransmitters and carriers of oxygen in the blood (hemoglobin).

Without protein, our tissues and organs could not exist. Our muscles bones, skin, and many other parts of the body contain significant amounts of protein. **Enzymes**, hormones, and antibodies are proteins.

Nucleic acids are large molecules made up of smaller molecules called **nucleotides. DNA** (deoxyribonucleic acid) transports and transmits genetic information. As you can tell from the name, DNA is a nucleic acid. Since nucleotides make up nucleic acids, they are considered the basis of reproduction and progression.

Life depends upon:
   a) The bond energy in molecules.
   b) The energy of protons.
   c) The energy of electrons.
   d) The energy of neutrons.

Which of the following elements is **NOT** found in carbohydrates?
   a) Carbon.
   b) Hydrogen.
   c) Oxygen.
   d) Sulfur.

Answer: A

Answer: D

Which of the following is a carbohydrate molecule?
   a) Amino acid.
   b) Glycogen.
   c) Sugar.
   d) Lipid.

What is Respiration?

Answer: C

Respiration is the metabolic opposite of photosynthesis. There are two types of respiration: **aerobic** (which uses oxygen) and **anaerobic** (which occurs without the use of oxygen).

What is Chlorophyll?

What is anaerobic respiration?

In order for photosynthesis to occur, plants require a specific molecule to capture sunlight. This molecule is called **chlorophyll**.

Anaerobic respiration is respiration that occurs WITHOUT the use of oxygen. It produces less energy than aerobic respiration produces, yielding only two molecules of ATP per glucose molecule Aerobic respiration produces 38 ATP per glucose molecule.

So, plants convert energy into matter and release oxygen gas – animals then absorb this oxygen gas in order to run their own metabolic reaction and, in the process, release carbon dioxide. That carbon dioxide is then absorbed by plants in the photosynthetic conversion of energy into matter. Everything comes full circle! This is called a **metabolic cycle.**

Which of the following is **NOT** true of enzymes?
a) Enzymes are lipid molecules.
b) Enzymes are not consumed in a biochemical reaction.
c) Enzymes are important in photosynthesis and respiration.
d) Enzymes speed up reactions and make them more efficient.

Plants appear green because chlorophyll:
a) Absorbs green light.
b) Reflects red light.
c) Absorbs blue light.
d) Reflects green light.

Answer: A

Answer: D

What is the name of the sugar molecule produced during photosynthesis?
- a) Chlorophyll.
- b) Glycogen.
- c) Glucose.
- d) Fructose.

What are the Kingdoms within the classification of organisms?

Answer: C

The five kingdoms are named as follows:

1. **Animalia**
2. **Plantae**
3. **Fungi**
4. **Protista**
5. **Monera**

What are heterotrophs?

Autotrophs store energy how?

Organisms that must eat preexisting organic matter (either plants or other animals) in order to sustain themselves.

Plants are multicellular organisms that use chlorophyll, which is held in specialized cellular structures called **chloroplasts,** to capture sunlight energy. Remember: photosynthesis! They then convert that sunlight energy into organic matter: their food. Because of this, most plants are referred to as **autotrophs** (self-feeders).

What are examples of organisms in the Fungi Kindom?

What are the Levels of Classification (Kingdom, Phylum.......)?

The most well-known examples of organisms in this Kingdom are mushrooms, yeasts, and molds.

Kingdom, **P**hylum, **C**lass, **O**rder, **F**amily, **G**enus, **S**pecies

Kingdom - insect, fish, bird, pig, dog, bear

Phylum - fish, bird, pig, dog, bear

Class - pig, dog, bear

Order - dog, bear

Family - panda, brown, grizzly

Genus - brown, grizzly

Species - grizzly

Which feature distinguishes those organisms in Kingdom Monera from those in other kingdoms? Organisms in Kingdom Monera:
- a) Contain specialized organelles.
- b) Contain a nucleus.
- c) Contain chloroplasts.
- d) Lack a nucleus.

The _____ contains organisms with both plant-and-animal-like characteristics?
- a) Animal Kingdom.
- b) Plant Kingdom.
- c) Fungi Kingdom.
- d) Monera Kingdom.

Answer: D

Answer: C

Which of the following kingdom's members are multicellular AND autotrophic?
   a) Fungi.
   b) Animalia.
   c) Protista.
   d) Plantae.

What are the three variations (shapes) bacteria are often found in?

Answer: D

Bacteria are normally found in three variations: **bacilli** (rod-shaped), **cocci** (sphere-shaped), and **spirilla** (spiral-shaped). Bacteria are widespread in all environments and are important participants within all ecosystems.

What are protists?

What do Saprophytic fungi consume?

Protists are very diversified and include organisms that range greatly in size – from single cells to considerably complex structures, some longer than 100 meters. Protists have a wide variety of reproductive and nutritional strategies, and their genetic material is enclosed within a nucleus. Even though protists are more simplistic than other organisms with cellular nuclei, they are not as primitive as bacteria.

Saprophytic fungi consume dead organic matter

How do fungi reproduce?

Which is the most numerous organism on Earth?
   a) Paramecium from the Protist Kingdom.
   b) Yeast from the Fungi Kingdom.
   c) Euglena from the Protist Kingdom.
   d) Bacteria from the Moneran Kingdom.

Fungi produce **spores** (reproductive structures) that are highly resistant to extreme temperatures and moisture levels. This gives them the ability to survive for a long time, even in aggressive environments. When their environments become more favorable, the spores **germinate** (sprout) and grow. Spores are able to travel to new areas, which spreads the organism.

Answer: D

Which kingdom contains organisms that are able to convert atmospheric nitrogen to nitrate?
- e) Animalia.
- f) Plantae.
- g) Monera.
- h) Protista.

What are Invertebrates?

Answer: C

Invertebrates are multicellular, have no back bone or cell walls, reproduce sexually, and are heterotrophic. They make up approximately 97% of the animal population

What are Vertebrates?

What is the difference between a plant cell and animal cell?

Vertebrates have well-developed internal skeletons, highly developed brains, an advanced nervous system, and an outer covering of protective cellular skin. They make up the remaining 3% of the animals.

In additional to a cell membrane, *plants* also have a **cell wall** which is necessary for structural support and protection. Animal cells do not contain a cell wall.

What is an Organelle?

What are Mitochondria?

Cells are filled with a gelatin-like substance called **protoplasm** which contains various structures called **organelles**; called so because they act like small versions of organs.

Spherical or rod-shaped organelles which carry out the reactions of aerobic respiration. They are the power generators of both plant and animal cells, because they convert oxygen and nutrients into ATP, the chemical energy that powers the cell's metabolic activities.

What are Ribosomes?

What are is the Golgi Apparatus?

Ribosomes are extremely tiny spheres that make proteins. These proteins are used either as enzymes or as support for other cell functions.

They are essential to the production of polysaccharides (carbohydrates), and made up of a layered stack of flattened sacs.

What are the three types of muscular tissue?

Describe Nervous tissue

1. **Cardiac** tissue, found in the heart.

2. **Smooth** tissue, located in the walls of hollow internal structures such as blood vessels, the stomach, intestines, and urinary bladder.

3. **Skeletal** (or striated) tissue, found in the muscles.

Nervous tissue consists of cells called **neurons.** Neurons specialize in making many connections with and transmitting electrical impulses to each other. The brain, spinal cord, and peripheral nerves are all made of nervous tissue.

What are the two types of reproduction?

Asexual reproduction occurs through a process known as ____?

One requires the exchange of genetic material between two organisms (**sexual reproduction**), and the other does not (**asexual reproduction**).

binary fission (or **bipartition**).
The cell first duplicates parts of itself before splitting into two separate, but identical, cells. Some organisms reproduce asexually using the process of **budding**, wherein an offshoot of their body grows into a complete organism.

In sexual reproduction, each parent produces a specialized cell called a _____ that contains half of his or her genetic information.

Male animals produce the smaller, more mobile gamete known as a _____?

Gamete

sperm cell

Females produce the larger, more sedentary gamete known as an _____?

When the two gametes come into contact, they fuse and combine their genetic information in a process known as _____?

egg cell

Fertilization (This can happen either externally or internally)

In sexually reproducing organisms, gametes come from which parent?
- a) Only the male.
- b) Only the female.
- c) Both the male and female.
- d) Neither.

What is the main difference between asexual and sexual reproduction?
- a) Asexual reproduction is only for aquatic organisms.
- b) Asexual reproduction is practiced only by plants.
- c) Humans are the only organisms that utilize sexual reproduction.
- d) Asexual reproduction does not require a mate.

Answer: C

Answer: D

Genes are made of _ _ _ ?

What is DNA?

DNA

DNA is a double helix (spiral) molecule that consists of two long, twisted strands of nucleic acids. Each of these strands are made of sugar and phosphate molecules, and are connected by pairs of chemicals called **nitrogenous bases** (just bases, for short).

What are the four types of DNA bases?

DNA molecules, and their important genetic material, are tightly packed around proteins called _____?

1. **Adenine (A)**
2. **Thymine (T)**
3. **Guanine (G)**
4. **Cytosine (C)**

histones

Human beings have __ pairs of chromosomes in every cell, for ___ chromosomes in total.

Male sex chromosomes are _ _ ?

Female sex chromosomes are _ _ ?

23 pairs for 46 total

Male: XY

Female: XX

Biologists refer to the genetic makeup of an organism as its _____?

The physical characteristics of an organism are known as its:
    a) Chromosomes.
    b) Genotype.
    c) DNA.
    d) Phenotype.

Genotype

Answer: D

Which of the following is **NOT** a nucleotide found in DNA?
- e) Uracil.
- f) Guanine.
- g) Cytosine.
- h) Thymine.

The shape of the DNA molecule is a:
- a) Single spiral.
- b) Double spiral.
- c) Straight chain.
- d) Bent chain.

Answer: A

Answer: B

What are the three main parts of the cardiovascular system?

The human heart has four chambers. What are they called?

three main parts: the heart (which is the pump in the system), the blood vessels providing a route for fluids in the system, and the blood which transports nutrients and oxygen and contains waste products.

right atrium, right ventricle, left atrium, and left ventricle

**When leaving the heart, blood travels through
_____.**

The _____ is the vein which brings blood from the body into the top right chamber of the heart.

arteries.

(HINT: To remember this, imagine that the "a" in "arteries" stands for "away". *A*rteries carry blood *a*way from the heart. On its way to the heart, blood travels through **veins.)**

superior vena cava

The right ventricle sends blood through the _____ to the lungs.

Blood picks up oxygen in the lungs and then is moved through the _____ back to the upper part of the heart.

pulmonary arteries

pulmonary veins

(HINT: But this time, it enters on the left side into the **left atrium.** Use that first-letter rule again to remember this: blood from the *l*ungs enters the *l*eft atrium.)

Arterioles lead to very small beds of tiny blood vessels called _____?

Things the Circulatory System Carries:

capillaries.

- Oxygen from the lungs to the body's cells.
- Carbon dioxide from the body's cells to the lungs.
- Nutrients from the digestive system to the cells.
- Waste products, other than carbon dioxide, to the liver and kidneys.
- Hormones and other messenger chemicals, from the glands and organs of their production to the body's cells.

Blood helps regulate our internal environment and keeps us in a generally constant state known as _____?

Blood is not a liquid; it is a _____?

Homeostasis

suspension (fluids containing particles suspended inside them).

Blood has two components._____ is the liquid part, and the solid _____ are suspended throughout.

Red blood cells contain a protein molecule called _____?

Plasma is liquid. Blood cells are solids.

Hemoglobin

The hemoglobin molecule binds with oxygen and carbon dioxide, thus providing the mechanism by which the red blood cells can carry these gases around the body.

Which of the following is NOT one of the chambers in the four-chambered vertebrate heart?
- a) Right atrium.
- b) Right ventricle.
- c) Left alveolar.
- d) Left ventricle.

Which of the following are the major components of blood?
- a) Proteins and lipids.
- b) Plasma and cells.
- c) Proteins and platelets.
- d) Dells and lipids.

Answer: C

Answer: B

Platelets perform which of the following functions?
 a) Blood clotting.
 b) Carrying oxygen.
 c) Carrying carbon dioxide.
 d) Disease protection.

Capillary beds occur between:
 a. Arteries and veins.
 b. Aortas and vena cavas.
 c. Arterioles and venules.
 d. Atria and ventricles.

Answer: A

Answer: C

What is the dome-shaped muscle located at the bottom of the lungs, controls breathing?

Humans breathe through their noses or mouths, which causes air to enter the _____ (upper part of the throat).

The diaphragm

pharynx

The trachea branches into two _____, two tubes which carry air into the lungs.

Bronchioles then lead to sac-like structures called _____, where the second function of the respiratory system – gas exchange – occurs.

Bronchi

alveoli

The lungs are very efficient at gas exchange because they have a:
   a) High mass.
   b) Low volume.
   c) High surface-area-to-volume ratio.
   d) Low surface-area-to-volume ratio.

What does the skeletal system do?

Answer: C

Skeletal systems provide structure, support, form, protection, and movement.

What is hematopoiesis?

Joints are where two bones come together; are all joints movable?

The bone marrow in animal skeletal systems performs **hematopoiesis** which is the manufacturing of both red blood cells and white blood cells.

No. Joints can be freely movable (elbow or knee), slightly movable (vertebrae in the back), or immovable (skull).

Which of the following is NOT a function of the skeletal system in animals?
- a) Transport fluids.
- b) Produce oil.
- c) Placement of internal organs.
- d) Production of blood cells.

Which of the following is true of bones?
- a) They contain nerves.
- b) Some are unbreakable.
- c) They are present in vertebrates.
- d) They directly touch each other at a joint.

Answer: B

Answer: C

_____ is a term used to describe an organism's response to changes, or stimuli, in its surroundings.

The functioning unit of the nervous system is the _____, a cell with structures capable of transmitting electrical impulses.

Irritability

neuron.

Neurons must be able to first receive information from internal or external sources, before integrating the signal and sending it to another neuron, gland, or muscle.

The _____ is an extension from the cell body which the nerve impulses travel along.

At the very end of the axon is the synaptic terminal, an area that contains chemical substances called _____.

Axon

Axons can be several feet in length, carrying signals from one end of the body to the other.

neurotransmitters

When an electrical nerve signal reaches the synaptic terminal, it causes neurotransmitters to be released. Neurotransmitters then move across the small space between the neuron and the next neuron (or gland or muscle). This small space is called the _____.

The central nervous system consists of the brain and _____.

synapse

(Once across the synapse, the neurotransmitter is received by the dendrites of another neuron (or the receptors on a gland or muscle) and then turned back into an electrical signal to be passed on.)

spinal cord (contained within the vertebral column or backbone). The brain integrates all the signals in the nervous system, and therefore is responsible for controlling every aspect of the body.

What is the main function of the PNS?

The somatic nervous system deals with motor functions such as……

The main function of the PNS is to connect the CNS to the limbs, organs, and **senses**.

Controls movement of all kinds, from fine motor skills to walking and running.

The autonomic nervous system works mostly without our conscious control and is often responsible for critical life functions such as….

The endocrine, or glandular, system controls what type of things in the human body?

breathing and heart rate

growth rate, feelings of hunger, body temperature, and more.

Name some of the major organs that run the endocrine system.

Which of the following is a part of the CNS?
    a) Autonomic nerves.
    b) Sympathetic nerves.
    c) Peripheral nerves.
    d) Spinal cord nerves.

The **pituitary gland**, the **pancreas**, the **ovaries** (only in females) and **testes** (only in males), the **thyroid** gland, the **parathyroid** gland, the **adrenal** glands, etc.

Answer: D

Which type of muscle tissue is consciously controlled?

Which type of muscle is under automatic control and is generally found in the internal organs, especially in the intestinal tract and in the walls of blood vessels?

Skeletal (or **striated**)
The muscle is attached to bones, and when it contracts, the bones move. Skeletal tissue also forms visible muscles, as well as much of the body mass.

Smooth

Muscle contraction is explained as the interaction between two necessary muscle proteins: thick bands of myosin and thin bands of _____.

Connective tissues known as _____ form a link between muscles and bones (whereas ligaments form a link between two bones).

Actin.

The thick myosin filaments have small knob-like projections that grab onto the thin actin filaments. As these knobs move slightly, they pull the actin filaments, which slide alongside the myosin filaments. This has the effect of shortening the muscle and thus causing a contraction.

Tendons

The contraction of a muscle causes an exertion of force upon the tendon, which then pulls its attached bone. This movement is synchronized by the central nervous system and results in movement.

The organs that make up the digestive tract are…..

Two "solid" digestive organs, the _____ and the _____, produce digestive juices.

mouth, esophagus, stomach, small intestine, large intestine (colon), rectum, and anus.

These organs are covered with a lining called the mucosa. In the mouth, stomach, and small intestine, the mucosa contains tiny glands which produce juices to help break down food.

liver and the pancreas

The _____ stores the liver's digestive juices until they are needed in the intestine. The circulatory and nervous systems are also important to the digestive system.

The movement of food molecules from one organ to the next, through *muscle action*, is called _____.

Gallbladder

peristalsis

When food in the stomach is partly digested and mixed with stomach acids, it is called _____.

From the stomach food molecules enter the first part of the small intestine called the _____.

chime

duodenum

The main function of the colon is to do what?

Solid waste is then stored in the _____ until it is excreted.

absorb water

rectum

Toxic wastes are carried by blood to the liver, where they are converted into _____.

The kidneys are complex filtering systems which maintain the proper levels of various life-supporting substances, including.......

Urea

sodium; potassium; chloride; calcium; glucose sugar; and amino acids.

The kidneys also help maintain blood pressure and the _____ level of the blood.

Alcohol consumption increases urination because it:
   a) Increases the amount of water in the body.
   b) Increases the action of antidiuretic hormone.
   c) Decreases the action of antidiuretic hormone.
   d) Stops water reabsorption.

Acidity (PH)

Answer: C

_____ is commonly defined as anything that takes up space and has mass.

_____ is the quantity of matter something possesses, and usually has a unit of weight associated with it.

Matter

Mass

A _____ occurs when an original substance is transformed into a new substance with different properties.

_____ properties are directly related to the amount of material being measured, such as weight and volume.

Chemical change
An example would be the burning of wood, which produces ash and smoke.

Extrinsic

An _____ is the ultimate particle of matter; it is the smallest particle of an element that still is a part of that element.

The center of an atom is called the _____.

Atom

Nucleus

The positively-charged particle of a nucleus is called a _____.

A _____ is the amount of substance that contains 6.02×10^{23} basic particles.

Proton

Mole

The weight of one mole of an element is called _____ ?

An _____ is a substance which cannot be broken down by chemical means.

Atomic weight

Element

_____ is the most abundant element in the Universe.

_____ is the second most abundant element, found in approximately 25% of all known matter.

Hydrogen

It is found in 75% of all matter known to exist.

Helium

Substances that contain more than one type of element are called _____.

A _____ consists of two or more substances that are not chemically bonded.

Compounds

Mixture

What is a Heterogeneous mixture?

A uniform, or homogenous, mixture of different molecules is called a _____.

Components of the mixture are not uniform; they sometimes have localized regions with different properties. For example: the different components of soup make it a heterogeneous mixture. Rocks, as well, are not uniform and have localized regions with different properties.

Solution

Which of the following is not a physical change?
   a) Melting of aspirin.
   b) Lighting a match.
   c) Putting sugar in tea.
   d) Boiling of antifreeze.

The identity of an element is determined by:
   a) The number of its protons and neutrons.
   b) The number of its neutrons.
   c) The number of its electrons.
   d) Its atomic mass.

Answer: B

Answer: A

True or False? When a match burns, some matter is destroyed.
   a) True.
   b) False.

What are Plasmas?

Answer: B (False)

Gases in which electrons are stripped from their nuclei.

What is Boyle's Law?

What is Charles's Law?

The volume of a given amount of gas at a constant temperature is inversely proportional to pressure. In other words; if the initial volume decreases by half, the pressure will double and vice versa. The representative equation is: $P_1V_1 = P_2V_2$.

The volume of a given amount of gas at a constant pressure is directly proportional to absolute (Kelvin) temperature. If the temperature of the gas increases, the volume of the gas also increases and vice versa. The representative equation is: $V_1/T_1 = V_2/T_2$.

What is Avogadro's Law?

The _____ assumes that gas molecules are very small compared to the distance between the molecules. Gas molecules are in constant, random motion; they frequently collide with each other and with the walls of whatever container they are in.

Equal volumes of all gases under identical conditions of pressure and temperature contain the same number of molecules. The molar volume of all ideal gases at 0° C and a pressure of 1 atm. is 22.4 liters.

Kinetic theory of gases

_____ is a chart which arranges the chemical elements in a useful, logical manner.

_____ is a force that is involved in all chemical behavior, including the chemical bonds which hold atoms together in order to form molecules, as well as those that hold molecules together to form all substances.

The Periodic Table

Electromagnetism

The two main types of bonds formed between atoms are _____ and _____.

Atoms do not always share the electrons equally, which results in a _____.

ionic bonds; covalent bonds

Polar covalent bond

Generally, how do atomic masses vary throughout the periodic table of the elements?
- a) They decrease from left to right and increase from top to bottom.
- b) They increase from left to right and increase bottom to top.
- c) They increase from left to right and increase top to bottom.
- d) They increase from right to left and decrease bottom to top.

Which one of the following is not a form of chemical bonding?
- a) Covalent bonding.
- b) Hydrogen bonding.
- c) Ionic bonding.
- d) Metallic bonding.

Answer: C

Answer: B

What are the acid characteristic properties?

What are the base characteristic properties?

- Have a sour taste.

- Speed up the corrosion, or rusting, of metals.

- Conduct electricity.

- Introduce H^+ cations into aqueous solutions.

These characteristic properties can be changed by the addition of a base.

- Have a bitter taste.

- Conduct electricity, when their solvent is water.

- Introduce OH^- ions into an aqueous solution.

The characteristic properties can be changed by the addition of an acid.

The acidity or basicity of a solution is expressed by _____.

The more acidic a solution, the _____ the pH is below 7.

pH values

Lower

A _____ is used to make a solution which exhibits very little change in its pH when small amounts of an acid or base are added to it.

One of the characteristic properties of an acid is that they introduce:
        a) Hydrogen ions.
        b) Hydroxyl ions.
        c) Hydride ions.
        d) Oxide ions.

Buffer

Answer: A

A solution with a pH of 12 is:
  a) Very acidic.
  b) Neutral.
  c) Very basic.
  d) You can't have a solution with a pH of 12.

Proper blood pH level for humans is:
  a. 7.0.
  b. 7.2.
  c. 7.6.
  d. 7.4.

Answer: C

Answer: D

_____ is a scalar quantity and is defined as distance divided by time.

_____ is a vector quantity that describes speed and the direction of travel.

Speed (Example: MPH)

Velocity

_____ is change in velocity divided by time; an object accelerates not only when it speeds up, but also when slowing down or turning.

The _____ of a falling object near the Earth is a constant 9.8m/s^2; therefore an object's magnitude increases as it falls and decreases as it rises.

Acceleration

Acceleration due to gravity

An object's _____ is its mass divided by its volume.

_____ arise when one object tries move over or around another; the frictional forces act in the opposite direction to oppose such a motion.

Density

Frictional forces

What is Conservation of Energy?

The energy stored within an object is called what?

Energy is neither created nor destroyed; it can be converted from one form to another (i.e. potential energy converted to kinetic energy), but the total amount of energy within the domain remains fixed.

Potential Energy

What is Kinetic energy?

_____ is the energy converted from one form to another, divided by the time needed to make the conversion.

The energy possessed because of an object's motion

Power

_____ is the inward force causing that object to move in the curved path.

If the centripetal force is the action, the (opposite) reaction is an outwardly-directed

Centripetal force

Centrifugal force

_____ is a measure of the work required to change the speeds in a collection of atoms or molecules.

_____ is a measure of the average kinetic energy of the atoms or molecules of a substance.

Heat

Temperature

A _____ is the amount of heat required to raise the temperature of 1 gram of water by 1 degree Celsius.

The _____ of a substance is the ratio of the amount of heat added to a substance, divided by the mass and the temperature change of the substance.

Calorie

Specific heat

What are the three common temperature scales?

What is Conduction?

Celsius, Fahrenheit, and Kelvin.

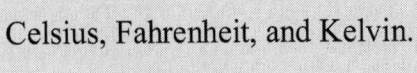

Heat transfer via conduction can occur in a substance of any phase (solid, liquid, or gas), but is mostly seen in solids.

What is Convection?

A wave's _____ is the distance between successive high points (crests) and low points (troughs).

Convection heat transfer occurs only in fluids (liquids and gases).

Wavelength

The _____ is the rate at which it moves.

_____ is the number of repetitions, or cycles, occurring per second.

Speed of a wave

Frequency

The _____ is the intensity (or strength) of the wave.

The speed of a_____ is approximately 331m/s at 0°C.

Amplitude

Speed of sound wave

The _____ scale is used to measure the loudness (amount of energy) of a sound wave.

Around every magnet there is a region in which its effects are felt, called its _____.

Decibel

Magnetic field

The magnetic field around a planet or a star is called the _____.

The strength of a magnet is measured in _____.

Magnetosphere

Teslas

The temperature at which all molecular motion stops is:
 a) −460 °C.
 b) −273 K.
 c) 0 K.
 d) 0C.

_____ is the amount of heat required to raise the temperature of 1 gram of water by 1 degree Celsius.
 a) Specific heat
 b) Heat of fusion
 c) Calorie
 d) Heat of vaporization

Answer: C

Answer: C

An object that has kinetic energy must be:
- a) Moving.
- b) Falling.
- c) At an elevated position.
- d) At rest.

A moving object has
- a) Velocity.
- b) Momentum.
- c) Energy.
- d) All of these.

Answer: A

Answer: D

Made in the USA
Lexington, KY
13 March 2015